TIME for KIDS

300 FANTASTIC FACTS!

SPACE

by WES LOCHER

PENGUIN YOUNG READERS LICENSES
An imprint of Penguin Random House LLC
1745 Broadway, New York, New York 10019

First published in the United States of America by Penguin Young Readers Licenses,
an imprint of Penguin Random House LLC, 2025

TIME for Kids © 2025 TIME USA, LLC. All Rights Reserved.

Penguin Random House values and supports copyright. Copyright fuels creativity, encourages diverse voices, promotes free speech, and creates a vibrant culture. Thank you for buying an authorized edition of this book and for complying with copyright laws by not reproducing, scanning, or distributing any part of it in any form without permission. You are supporting writers and allowing Penguin Random House to continue to publish books for every reader. Please note that no part of this book may be used or reproduced in any manner for the purpose of training artificial intelligence technologies or systems.

Visit us online at penguinrandomhouse.com.

Library of Congress Cataloging-in-Publication Data is available.

Manufactured in China

ISBN 9780593888025   10 9 8 7 6 5 4 3 2 1 TOPL

Design by Hsiao-Pin Lin

The publisher does not have any control over and does not assume any responsibility for author or third-party websites or their content.

. . . .

Photo credits: Cover: Alamy: (astronaut) RH Ingram_AAR/Ingram Publishing. **Getty Images:** (front) dima_zel/iStock, (spine) Elen11/iStock. **Interior: Alamy:** 6: RH Ingram_AAR/Ingram Publishing; 15: (top) Pictorial Press Ltd; 28: Geopix. **Getty Images:** 1: AlexLMX/iStock; 3: NiseriN/iStock; 5: Elen11/iStock; 7: Oselote/iStock; 8: alex-mit/iStock; 10: alxpin/E+; 11: fbxx/iStock; 12: Ilia Smirnov/iStock; 13: The Image Bank; 14: (background) dima_zel/iStock, (inset) Drbouz/iStock; 16–17: peepo/iStock; 20–21: Alones Creative/iStock; 23: Paopano/iStock; 24–25: Stocktrek/Photodisc; 26–27: Alones Creative/iStock; 29: happywhale/iStock; 30: 3DSculptor/iStock; 33: Paul Campbell/iStock; 34–35: peepo/iStock; 36–37: dottedhippo/iStock; 39: Gwengoat/iStock; 40: PaulFleet/iStock; 43: junak/iStock; 44–45: CRAIG TAYLOR/iStock; 46: forplayday/iStock; 47: buradaki/iStock; 48–49: UniqueMotionGraphics/iStock; 50, 52–53, 54–55: buradaki/iStock; 56: Stocktrek Images; 57: Nastco/iStock; 58: adventtr/E+; 60–61: digitalmazdoor/iStock; 62–63: dottedhippo/iStock; 66–67: (background), (inset) Stocktrek Images; 68–69: forplayday/iStock; 70–71: (background) dottedhippo/iStock, (inset) Gwengoat/iStock; 72: Ploystock/iStock; 74–75: dottedhippo/iStock; 76–77: alexaldo/iStock; 78: Stocktrek Images; 79: Johannes Gerhardus Swanepoel/iStock; 80–81: (background) dottedhippo/iStock; 82: 3000ad/iStock; 83: Ianm35/iStock; 84: Mahdi Langari/iStock; 86–87: buradaki/iStock; 88–89: alexaldo/iStock; 90: Mahdi Langari/iStock; 92–93: Ianm35/iStock; 94–95: dottedhippo/iStock; 97: dima_zel/iStock; 98–99: photovideostock/iStock; 100: teekid/iStock; 104: narvikk/E+; 106–107: JoZtar/iStock; 109: adventtr/E+; 110–111: aryos/E+; 112–113: Thomas Faull/iStock; 114–115: giemgiem/iStock; 118: vitacop5/iStock; 120–121, 123: dima_zel/iStock; 124–125: murat4art/iStock; 126: Eduard-Harkonen/iStock; 128–129: Naeblys/iStock; 131: Stocktrek Images; 132–133: teddybearpicnic/iStock; 135: PaulPaladin/iStock; 136: Pitris/iStock; 139: angelinast/iStock; 140–141: AlxeyPnferov/iStock; 142–143: kyoshino/iStock; 145: sololos/E+; 146: murat4art/iStock; 147: janiecbros/iStock; 148–149: imaginima/iStock; 150–151: Wirestock/iStock; 153: Maximusnd/iStock; 154–155: Nzoka John/iStock; 156–157: peepo/iStock; 158: Ianm35/iStock; 159: cemagraphics/E+. **Wikimedia Commons:** 15: (bottom) NASA; 18: NASA; 41: Thomas Murray (public domain); 65: NASA; 80: (inset) NASA/JPL-Caltech/Space Science Institute; 103: NASA; 117: European Southern Observatory (ESO) (CC BY 4.0).

INTRODUCTION

The exact age of our universe is a mystery. Scientists estimate that the universe—full of planets, stars, asteroids, and other wonders—is between 13.71 and 13.83 billion years old. Of course, that's just an approximation. Our home planet of Earth is estimated to be 4.5 billion years old, and humans have been around for about three hundred thousand of those years.

Humans have studied the skies for centuries, but we've only been actually exploring space since 1957. That's when the Sputnik satellite was launched by the Soviet Union. Though humans have existed for hundreds of thousands of years, the majority of what we know about our galaxy (and beyond) has been learned in the past seventy years or so. But in that short time, we have learned much.

We've learned about stars and constellations. We've learned about neighboring galaxies. We've constructed and launched massive rockets that defy gravity. We've put humans on the moon and created technology to help them survive. We've built space stations that circle the Earth and satellites that photograph distant planets. We've built telescopes that allow scientists to see across the cosmos, and in the darkness, we've discovered planets previously unknown and unseen.

Despite these discoveries and successes, there's still a lot that we *don't* know. Scientists are constantly learning exciting new things about space and our place in the universe. There is always more to discover!

Meanwhile, what follows are three hundred fun facts on what we *do* know about outer space.

Prepare to learn about the amazing planets in our home solar system—Mercury, Venus, Earth, Mars, Jupiter, Saturn, Uranus, and Neptune. Hear exciting details about our moon and sun. Read about brave astronauts who explored space and the space stations, telescopes, and satellites that help scientists learn more each day. Learn about dazzling asteroids, meteors, and comets that fly through the cosmos at impossible speeds and black holes that feed on stars and planets that wander too close. Soon you'll see why space is such a mysterious, dangerous, beautiful, and amazing place.

GENERAL FACTS ABOUT SPACE

Outer space begins just **SIXTY-TWO** miles away from the Earth's surface.

Space is very cold: approximately **-459** degrees Fahrenheit.

Outer space is **SILENT.**

Scientists believe that, in our known universe, there are more than **TWO TRILLION** galaxies—and each galaxy contains billions of stars and their own solar systems!

THE MILKY WAY is the name of the galaxy that contains our solar system.

Within the Milky Way are more than **ONE HUNDRED BILLION** planets and as many as **FOUR HUNDRED BILLION** stars.

Scientists think the Milky Way galaxy is close to **FOURTEEN BILLION** years old.

Astronomers estimate that our **galaxy** has more than three hundred million **HABITABLE PLANETS.** *Habitable* means that life can survive there. Habitable planets require **liquid water, energy,** and **nutrients.**

Our **solar system** consists of **EIGHT PLANETS** that orbit around the sun.

Space is mostly **EMPTY**. The many galaxies, planets, moons, stars, comets, and asteroids are very **FAR APART**. Even though space is mostly empty, it is also incredibly *huge*. That's why so many things can fit within it, even if they are far apart.

The Milky Way gets its name from the hazy or **"MILKY"** appearance of the groups of stars that can be seen from the Earth's surface.

A **LIGHT-YEAR** is the distance that light travels in one year. One light-year is about **5.88 TRILLION** miles.

The Milky Way is **ONE HUNDRED THOUSAND** light-years wide. That means it would take one hundred thousand years to travel from one end of the galaxy to the other while moving at the speed of light.

If we were to try to travel from one end of the Milky Way to the other at the speed our current spacecraft can go, it would take more than **1.7 BILLION YEARS.**

FACTS ABOUT SPACE EXPLORATION

The National Aeronautics and Space Administration **(NASA)** was founded in 1958.

Humans have been traveling into space since **1961.**

THE SOVIET SPACE PROGRAM, in the Soviet Union, ran from 1955 to 1991. It was replaced by the Roscosmos State Corporation in 1992.

FRUIT FLIES were the first animals in space. The USA launched them aboard a rocket in 1947.

In 1957, the Soviet Union launched the **first dog** into space. Her name was **LAIKA.**

The USA sent a **chimpanzee** named **HAM THE ASTROCHIMP** on a sixteen-minute ride to space in 1961 to better understand the effects of space travel on humans. This is because the DNA sequence of a human and a chimpanzee is more than **98 percent** identical.

A trained person who travels into space is called an **ASTRONAUT** in the United States.

A trained person who travels into space is called a **COSMONAUT** in Russia.

In China, astronauts are called **TAIKONAUTS** (say: TIE-ko-nauts).

In France, they are called **SPATIONAUTES** (say: spa-sio-NAUTS).

In Greek, the word *astronaut* means **"STAR SAILOR."**

The **first human** in space was Soviet cosmonaut **YURI GAGARIN.** He went into Earth's orbit in 1961. His journey to space lasted less than two hours.

Only a few weeks after Yuri Gagarin's flight, **ALAN SHEPARD** became the **first American** and second person ever to travel into space.

The **first two women** to go into space were Russian cosmonauts. Their names were **VALENTINA TERESHKOVA** (who went in 1963) and **SVETLANA SAVITSKAYA** (who went in 1982).

The **first American woman** and third woman worldwide to go into space was **SALLY RIDE,** who completed her first mission in 1983.

The record for the longest consecutive amount of time in space belongs to **Russian cosmonaut VALERI POLYAKOV.** He spent **437** days orbiting Earth. He entered space on January 8, 1994, and did not return to Earth until March 22, 1995.

Russian cosmonaut **GENNADY PADALKA** holds the record for most overall time spent in space. If you add up all his missions, he has spent a total of **879** days in space.

American astronaut **SCOTT KELLY** has spent more than **500** days in space. When he returned to Earth after a 340-day stay on the International Space Station, scientists studied how being in space affected his body by comparing him to his twin brother, who stayed on Earth.

Space shuttles travel at more than **SEVENTEEN THOUSAND** miles per hour and reach outer space in about **EIGHT** minutes.

When a **rocket** launches, it burns up to **ELEVEN THOUSAND POUNDS** of fuel every second. This is two million times as fast as a car burns through fuel.

To escape Earth's gravity, a rocket must travel at seven miles per second, or twenty-five thousand miles per hour. This speed is known as **ESCAPE VELOCITY.** If a rocket goes too slowly, gravity will pull it back down to Earth.

After astronauts use the bathroom, their poop is shot into space. It then burns up upon reentry into **EARTH'S ATMOSPHERE,** disappearing forever.

Inside a space suit's helmet is a small **VELCRO** patch that astronauts use to scratch their faces if they get itchy.

The cargo carried on a spacecraft is very valuable and can cost up to **$43,000** per pound. Cargo items might include a satellite, telescope, or supplies. A spacecraft can also carry new people coming to join the crew on the International Space Station.

FACTS ABOUT SPACE STATIONS

In 1971, the **Soviet Union** launched the first space station, called **SALYUT** (say: sa-LUTE). Salyut stayed in orbit for **175 days** before falling back to Earth, landing in pieces in the Pacific Ocean.

In 1973, the **USA** launched its first space station, called **SKYLAB.** It stayed in Earth's orbit for just over **six years.** At the end of its mission, the space station broke up in Earth's atmosphere. Pieces were found in Australia and the Indian Ocean.

25

In 1998, the **INTERNATIONAL SPACE STATION (ISS)** was launched. This feat required the USA, Russia, Japan, Europe, and Canada to all work together as a team.

It took **TEN YEARS** and more than thirty space missions to assemble the ISS.

The ISS cost **$150 BILLION** to build. It is the most expensive thing ever constructed by humans.

The ISS orbits the Earth at **17,500** miles per hour.

As of the spring of 2024, **280** different astronauts have visited the International Space Station.

The ISS circles the Earth every **NINETY MINUTES.** Astronauts on board see sixteen sunrises and sunsets every day.

The **ISS** is the size of a **FOOTBALL FIELD.**

In Earth's gravity, the **ISS** would weigh about **460 TONS.**

The **ISS** contains **SIX LABORATORIES** where astronauts conduct experiments.

Astronauts on the **ISS** float around and appear to be **WEIGHTLESS.** This is because the space station is in a slow, constant free fall toward Earth.

28

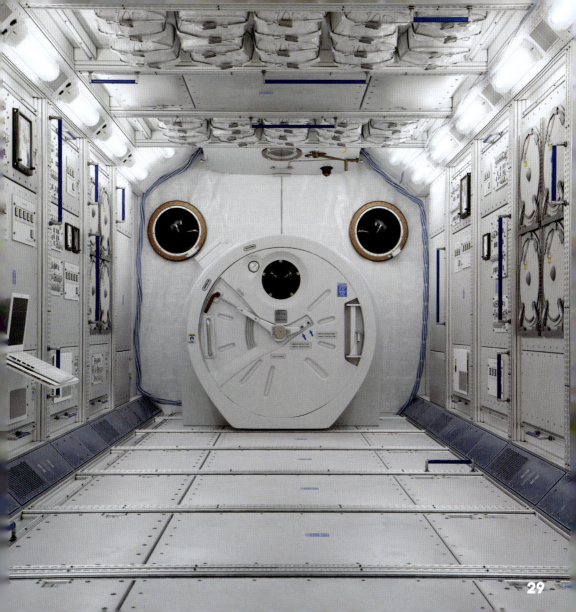

On the ISS, astronauts drink water recycled from their **BREATH, SWEAT,** and **URINE.** Don't worry—thanks to the recycling process, the water is safe and tastes normal!

On a clear night, the ISS can be **SEEN** without a telescope. It looks like a bright, fast-moving star.

The International Space Station will remain in Earth's orbit until the end of **2030.**

NINE new space stations are currently being planned to take the place of the ISS.

The **gravity** on Earth causes human's spines to press together. In space, astronauts can grow an average of **TWO INCHES** taller until they return to Earth. Can you imagine if you were suddenly two inches taller?

Side effects of staying in space for a long time include weakened **MUSCLES** and a decrease in **BONE DENSITY.** Bones with low density have more tiny holes in them, which cause them to be weaker and break more easily.

Astronauts on the ISS must **EXERCISE** daily to help keep their muscles strong.

A **space suit** on Earth weighs more than **THREE HUNDRED POUNDS.** In space, it weighs nothing.

A single **space suit** costs around **$500 MILLION** to make.

It takes an astronaut about **THIRTY MINUTES** to put on a **space suit.**

Russian cosmonaut **ALEKSEI LEONOV** performed the first-ever space walk in 1965.

An **EXTRAVEHICULAR ACTIVITY,** or EVA, is any activity done by an astronaut outside a spacecraft. When an astronaut performs a space walk, they are performing an extravehicular activity. Astronauts must wear space suits when they are not in a spacecraft.

The longest space walk in history happened in 2001. American astronauts **SUSAN HELMS** and **JIM VOSS** spent eight hours and fifty-six minutes repairing the outside of the ISS.

FACTS ABOUT ASTEROIDS, METEORS, AND COMETS

Asteroids are rocky objects that float through space. They are often made of **ROCK** and **METAL**.

The term *asteroid* was first used by astronomer William Herschel in 1802. *Asteroid* means **"STARLIKE."**

Most **asteroids** in our solar system come from a large group that floats around between the planets **MARS** and **JUPITER.**

Even if you gathered up all the asteroids in our solar system, they wouldn't be as large as Earth's **MOON.**

The largest asteroid ever recorded was 585 miles long. That is longer than the distance between New York City and Toledo, Ohio. The asteroid was named **CERES.** Today, however, scientists consider Ceres a dwarf planet, not an asteroid.

Scientists believe **ORGANIC LIFE** could exist on the Ceres asteroid because water has been seen on its surface.

When a floating object in space is made of frozen gas, dust, rock, and water, it is called a **COMET.**

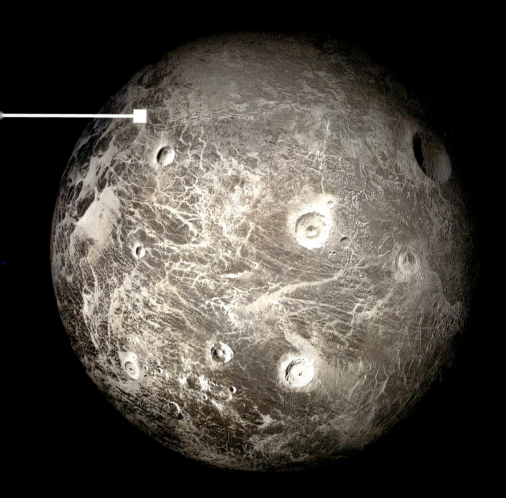

Scientists believe that **comets** are leftover material from the creation of our **SOLAR SYSTEM.**

Most comets are more than **SIX MILES** wide.

Comets leave behind visible streams of dust and gas called **TAILS**.

The most famous comet is **HALLEY'S COMET.** It is named after astronomer Edmond Halley.

Halley's comet can be seen from Earth every **SEVENTY-SIX** years. It will next be visible in **2061**.

According to historical records, **Halley's comet** was first spotted in **240 BC.**

Other famous **comets** are **HALE-BOPP,** discovered in 1995, and **HYAKUTAKE,** first seen in 1996.

There are more than **ONE TRILLION** comets flying around our solar system.

A **METEOROID** is a piece of an asteroid or comet that has broken off and floats through space. Meteoroids can be as small as a pebble.

Meteoroids sometimes **COLLIDE** with satellites and space stations. The ISS has more than one hundred shields to protect itself.

Meteoroids travel as fast as **TWENTY-SIX** miles per second.

A **METEOR** is a piece of an asteroid that enters Earth's atmosphere—where it usually burns up before reaching the ground.

Meteors are also known as **SHOOTING STARS.** So when a person wishes on a shooting star, they are actually looking at a meteor flying.

A **METEOR SHOWER** occurs when many meteors enter the Earth's atmosphere over the course of several hours.

Approximately **THIRTY** meteor showers can be seen from Earth every year.

A **METEORITE** is a piece of a meteor that survives the trip through Earth's atmosphere and hits the ground.

Around **SEVENTEEN THOUSAND** meteorites reach Earth's surface every year.

By the time they touch down, most meteorites are the size of a **PEBBLE.**

The rarest meteorites come from the moon and Mars and sell for more than **$1,000** per gram. For an idea of how small one gram is, it's about the weight of a single raisin.

FACTS ABOUT MERCURY

Mercury is the **SMALLEST** planet in our solar system and the closest to the sun.

Mercury is named after the Roman **MESSENGER GOD.**

If you stood on **Mercury's** surface, the sun would look **THREE TIMES** larger than it does from the Earth, and the sunlight would be **SEVEN TIMES** brighter.

A year on **Mercury** lasts **EIGHTY-EIGHT** days, or about three months in Earth time. This is because it takes about eighty-eight days for **Mercury** to orbit around the sun one time.

Scientists believe that **Mercury** is mostly made of **METALS** such as **iron** and **nickel**.

Instead of an atmosphere (thick gases that surround a planet), Mercury has a thin **EXOSPHERE** made of oxygen, sodium, hydrogen, helium, and potassium.

While Mercury is the closest planet to the sun, its surface temperature at night is an extremely cold **-290** degrees Fahrenheit.

The temperature on Mercury rises to a very hot **800** degrees Fahrenheit during the day.

Mercury is **FORTY-EIGHT MILLION** miles away from Earth at the closest point in their orbits. When the two planets are at their closest, it would still take forty days to travel on a modern spacecraft from Earth to Mercury.

FACTS ABOUT VENUS

Venus is the **SECOND** planet from the sun and the closest planet to Earth.

Venus is the **THIRD-BRIGHTEST** object in Earth's sky, after the sun and the moon.

A single day on **Venus** is as long as **243** days on Earth. That is how long it takes **Venus** to rotate just once on its axis.

Venus is named after the Roman goddess of **LOVE** and **BEAUTY.**

Venus has **NO MOONS** of its own.

While most planets rotate counterclockwise, both **Venus** and **Uranus** spin in the **OPPOSITE** direction.

Scientists think the surface of **Venus** is about **500 MILLION** years old, which is much younger than Earth's surface. The oldest rocks and crystals on Earth are more than **3.5 billion years old.**

The atmosphere on **Venus** is made up of **CARBON DIOXIDE** and thick **ACID CLOUDS.**

The surface of **Venus** is **867** degrees Fahrenheit. Its dense atmosphere holds in heat, making it the **HOTTEST PLANET** in our solar system.

Venus is home to more than **85,000** **volcanoes.**

It snows **METAL** and rains **ACID** on **Venus.** Can you imagine a snowman made out of metal?

FACTS ABOUT EARTH

Earth, where we live, is the **THIRD** planet from the sun in our solar system.

Scientists have calculated that the Earth is around **4.5 BILLION** years old.

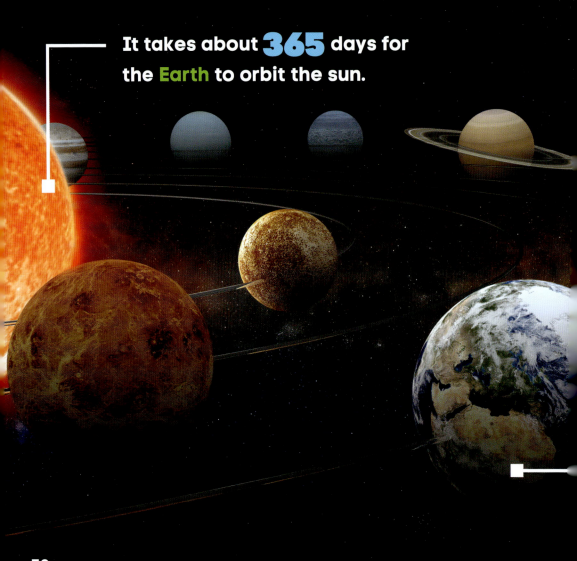

It takes about 365 days for the Earth to orbit the sun.

Earth spins at around **ONE THOUSAND** miles per hour and orbits the sun at **SIXTY-SEVEN THOUSAND** miles per hour.

Earth is the only planet with large bodies of **LIQUID WATER.**

It takes **TWENTY-FOUR** hours for **Earth** to spin around once on its axis. When the area where you live is facing the sun, it's **daytime.** When it's facing away, it's **nighttime.** That's why our days are twenty-four hours long!

Earth is the **FIFTH-LARGEST** planet in our solar system. It is smaller than Jupiter, Saturn, Uranus, and Neptune.

Earth is the only planet in our solar system known to support **LIFE.**

The **Earth's** atmosphere holds in **HEAT** from the sun to keep us **warm**. It also holds **OXYGEN** so we can **breathe**.

Earth's atmosphere has **FIVE LAYERS: troposphere, stratosphere, mesosphere, thermosphere,** and **exosphere.**

Earth has one moon, simply called **THE MOON.** It takes about a month for the moon to orbit around the Earth.

Each year, it takes Earth fractions of a second longer to complete its spin. Because of this, our days will get **LONGER** over time.

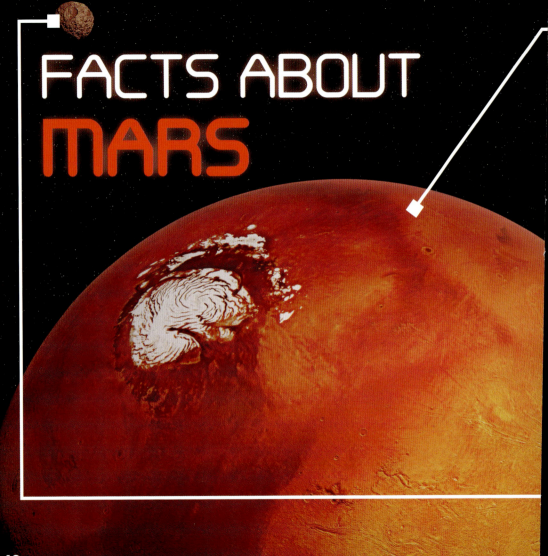

FACTS ABOUT MARS

- Mars gets its nickname the **"RED PLANET"** because it is covered in red rust.

Mars is the **SECOND-SMALLEST** planet in the solar system after Mercury.

Mars is about **HALF THE SIZE** of Earth.

Mars was named for the Roman god of **WAR.**

Mars has **TWO MOONS:** Deimos and Phobos.

Mars is the **FOURTH** planet away from the sun.

If you jumped on Mars, you would go **THREE TIMES HIGHER** than you do on Earth thanks to Mars's lower level of gravity.

If you watched the sunset from the surface of Mars, it would appear **BLUE.**

NASA has sent **FIVE ROBOTIC VEHICLES** to Mars. These rovers were called Sojourner, Spirit, Opportunity, Curiosity, and Perseverance.

SOJOURNER, the first rover sent to Mars, was about the size of a microwave.

There is a 2,500-mile-long canyon on Mars called **VALLES MARINERIS.** It's nearly as long as the entire United States and five times deeper than the Grand Canyon.

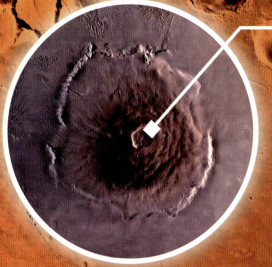

Mars is home to the tallest mountain ever discovered, called **OLYMPUS MONS.** It is sixteen miles tall—eleven miles taller than Earth's Mount Everest.

A day on Mars is just **THIRTY-NINE** minutes longer than a day on Earth.

If you stood on the equator of Mars at noon, your feet would be warm, but your head would be freezing cold. The atmosphere on Mars is **MUCH THINNER** than the one we have on Earth, and heat escapes the surface of Mars much faster.

FACTS ABOUT JUPITER

Jupiter is the **LARGEST** planet in our solar system. It's bigger than all the other planets combined.

Jupiter is the **FIFTH** planet from the sun. Its neighbors are Mars and Saturn.

The temperature on **Jupiter** is about **-166** degrees Fahrenheit.

Jupiter is **ELEVEN** times the width of Earth. If Earth were the size of a nickel, Jupiter would be as large as a basketball.

Jupiter has **NINETY-FIVE** moons.

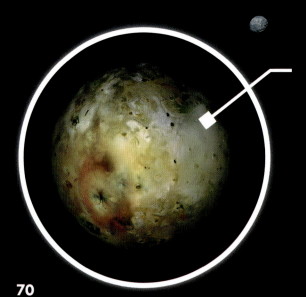

Jupiter's third-largest moon, called **IO,** has hundreds of volcanoes on its surface. When they erupt, they shoot fire up to 250 miles into the sky.

Because of its size, early astronomers named Jupiter after the KING of the Roman gods.

Scientists believe that it rains **DIAMONDS** on both Jupiter and Saturn.

Jupiter is the **FASTEST-SPINNING** planet in our solar system. It takes **TEN** hours to complete a full rotation, which means one day on Jupiter is ten hours long.

Jupiter is known as a **GAS** giant because it is made up of swirling dust and gas. It has no known solid surface.

Jupiter has all the same features as a **STAR.** The planet simply did not grow large enough to heat up like our sun.

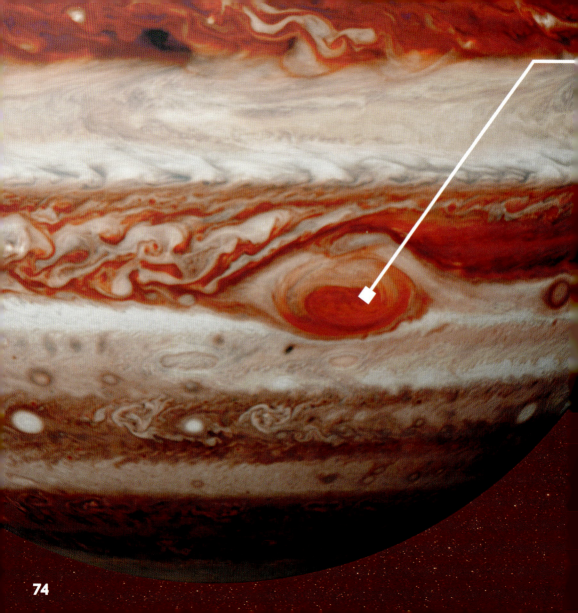

Jupiter is best known for its **GREAT RED SPOT,** which is the solar system's longest ongoing storm. It has been observed for more than three hundred years.

The **STORM** happening inside **Jupiter's** Great Red Spot is larger than the entire Earth.

Ancient astronomers knew about **Jupiter** because it can be seen in the sky like a **STAR,** without the use of advanced telescopes.

In 2011, three **LEGO MINIFIGURES** representing the Roman god **Jupiter,** his wife **Juno,** and famed astronomer **Galileo Galilei** were put on a space probe bound for Jupiter. Since 2016, the minifigures have been orbiting Jupiter inside the Juno space probe.

FACTS ABOUT SATURN

Saturn is the **SIXTH** planet from the sun.

Saturn is the **SECOND-LARGEST** planet in our solar system.

Saturn is named after the Roman god of **WEALTH** and **FARMING.**

Saturn has **146** moons. All of them are **FROZEN**.

One of Saturn's moons, called **IAPETUS**, has one icy half and one very dark half. It looks a bit like the yin and yang symbol (*taijitu*).

Like Jupiter, Saturn is made of **GAS** and has no solid surface.

Saturn is the only planet in our solar system that could **FLOAT** in water.

Saturn is surrounded by **EIGHT MAIN RINGS**.

78

Saturn's rings are made up of many small pieces of **ROCK.** The pieces came from comets, asteroids, and moons that were pulled apart by the planet's extremely strong gravity.

Saturn's major rings have a diameter of **170,000** miles. If you were running six miles per hour, it would take you a little more than 1,180 days to run around one ring.

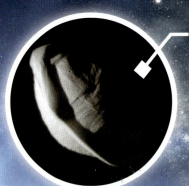

PAN, one of Saturn's moons, is shaped like a walnut.

Saturn's winds are some of the strongest in our solar system, blowing as fast as **1,100** miles per hour.

For more than ten years, NASA's **CASSINI** spacecraft flew around Saturn and took photographs of the planet.

When the Cassini spacecraft ran out of fuel in 2017, scientists made it dive toward Saturn as its final act. It burned up in Saturn's **UPPER ATMOSPHERE.** A lot of spacecraft never return to Earth.

FACTS ABOUT URANUS

Uranus is the SEVENTH planet from the sun in our solar system.

Uranus is named after the Greek god of the SKY.

Uranus has a solid **CORE** buried deep within layers of icy fluids and gas.

Uranus is the **COLDEST** planet in our solar system, with temperatures as low as **-371** degrees Fahrenheit.

Unlike most planets, Uranus spins at an **EXTREME TILT.** Scientists believe this is due to a large collision with an asteroid that happened long ago that caused it to start spinning a different way—almost as if the planet was pushed by the asteroid.

If we were able to smell the gas around Uranus, it would smell like **ROTTEN EGGS.** This is because of the hydrogen sulfide in the atmosphere.

Through a telescope, **Uranus** looks like a featureless **BLUE BALL** floating in space.

Most of the data scientists have on **Uranus** was collected by NASA's **VOYAGER 2** space probe in 1986. It is very difficult for spacecraft to reach **Uranus** since it is so far from Earth, and Voyager 2 was one of the few spacecraft able to make it that great distance.

One day on **Uranus** lasts **SEVENTEEN** Earth hours, but one year on **Uranus** takes **EIGHTY-FOUR** years on Earth. Why? **Uranus** spins on its axis quicker than Earth but takes much longer than Earth to orbit the sun.

Uranus has **THIRTEEN** rings. The largest and brightest is called the **EPSILON RING.**

FACTS ABOUT NEPTUNE

Neptune is the EIGHTH planet from the sun and the most distant of our known planets.

One day on Neptune lasts SIXTEEN Earth hours.

Neptune has SIXTEEN moons.

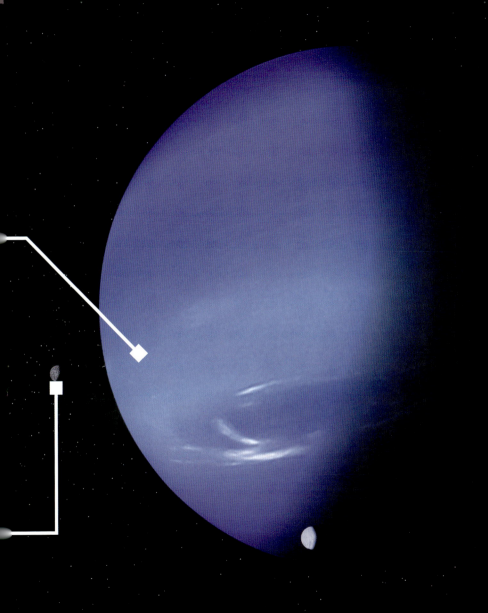

Neptune has a solid center the size of Earth, but the planet is covered in thick, icy **FOG** made of water and poisonous gas that makes it look larger.

Neptune is named after the Roman god of the **SEA**.

It would take a spacecraft more than **EIGHTEEN YEARS** to get to Neptune from Earth.

One of Neptune's moons, named **TRITON**, orbits the planet in reverse of all the others.

Over time, Triton is getting **CLOSER** to **Neptune**. One day, **Neptune's** gravity will tear Triton apart.

Neptune completes an orbit of our sun once every **165** Earth years. That means a year on **Neptune** is as long as 165 years on Earth.

If you could visit **Neptune**, you would find it to be incredibly cold, dark, and windy. It is **-330** degrees Fahrenheit there!

Neptune has **FIVE** main rings that we know of—Galle, Leverrier, Lassell, Arago, and Adams.

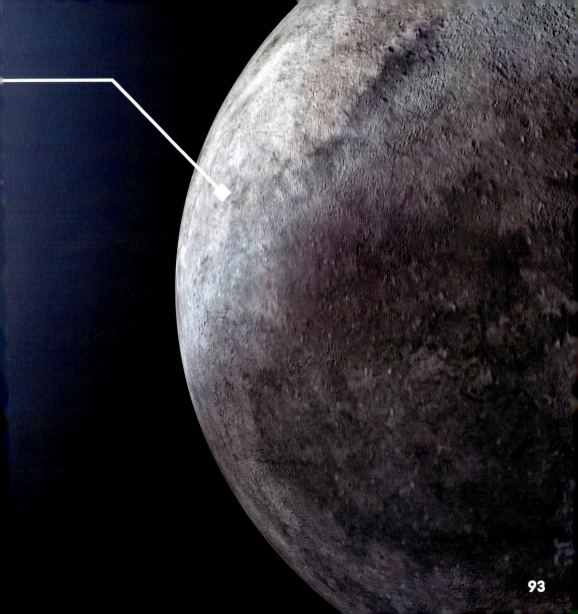

FACTS ABOUT PLUTO

Pluto was considered the **NINTH** planet in our solar system until it was reclassified as a **dwarf planet** in 2006.

Pluto has FIVE moons: Charon, Styx, Nix, Kerberos, and Hydra.

Pluto is **3.6 BILLION** miles from our sun.

Pluto is just **1,400** miles wide, smaller than the United States.

Pluto is named after the Roman god of the **UNDERWORLD.**

Icy mountains rising as high as **ELEVEN THOUSAND** feet tall have been seen on **Pluto's** surface.

Pluto isn't the only **DWARF PLANET** in our solar system. Others include **Ceres, Makemake, Haumea,** and **Eris.**

FACTS ABOUT THE MOON

The moon is a DUSTY ROCK that is about a quarter the size of Earth.

Scientists believe that part of the moon was originally a piece of EARTH that broke off.

While the moon seems to shine at night, it does not actually produce any light of its own. Instead, it REFLECTS the light of the sun.

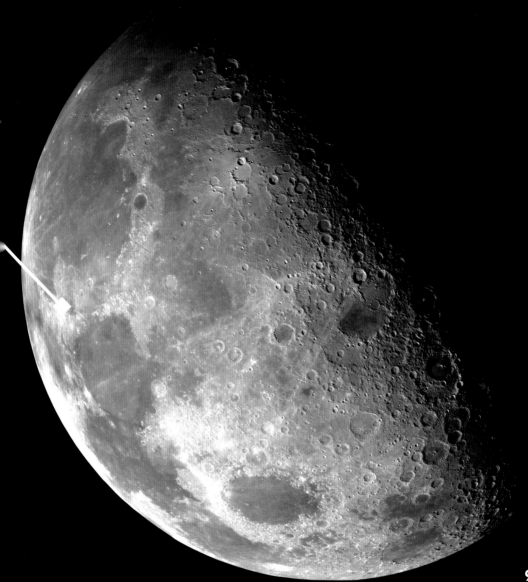

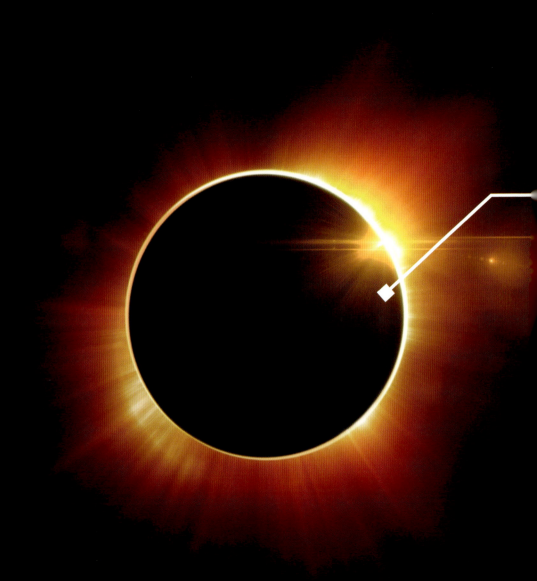

A **LUNAR ECLIPSE** happens when Earth passes between the sun and the moon, casting a shadow onto the moon.

A **SOLAR ECLIPSE** occurs when the moon passes between the sun and the Earth, casting a shadow on the Earth's surface and blocking our view of the sun.

The moon is called **LUNA** in Latin, which is where the term *lunar* comes from.

While it looks like a perfect circle from Earth, the moon is actually shaped more like a **LEMON.**

The **first humans** to walk on **the moon** were American astronauts **NEIL ARMSTRONG** and **BUZZ ALDRIN** as part of the Apollo 11 space mission in 1969.

A total of **TWELVE** astronauts have walked on **the moon.**

Astronaut **CHARLES DUKE** left a picture of his family on **the moon** in 1972.

American astronauts have played **SPORTS** on **the moon.** In 1971, Alan Shepard hit a **golf ball** while Edgar Mitchell threw a staff like a **javelin.**

The moon doesn't smell like cheese at all. Astronauts say it smells more like **WET ASHES** or **GUNPOWDER.**

Since there is no wind on the moon, the **FOOTPRINTS** left behind by astronauts will stay on its surface forever.

The moon cannot retain heat because it has no atmosphere. During the daytime, the moon's surface can reach **260** degrees Fahrenheit. During the nighttime, the moon's surface can drop to **-280** degrees Fahrenheit.

Each year the moon moves farther away from Earth by **ONE INCH.**

FACTS ABOUT THE SUN

Our sun is **865,000** miles wide, which is 109 times wider than Earth. More than a million Earths could fit inside the sun.

Scientists believe the sun is about **4.6 BILLION** years old.

The sun has been getting **BRIGHTER** over time. Billions of years ago, the sun was dimmer than it is right now.

It takes light from the sun EIGHT MINUTES AND TWENTY SECONDS to reach Earth's surface.

The sun is so large, it makes up more than **99 PERCENT** of the mass in our solar system.

The sun is the only **STAR** in our solar system. The stars you see at night are all part of our Milky Way galaxy. But there are a *lot* of galaxies filled with stars outside the Milky Way.

Our sun is made up of about 70 percent **HYDROGEN** and about 28 percent **HELIUM.**

The surface temperature of the sun is **TEN THOUSAND** degrees Fahrenheit. Scientists believe its core temperature is closer to **TWENTY-SEVEN MILLION** degrees Fahrenheit.

Once the sun has burned all its hydrogen, it will burn helium for **130 MILLION** more years. During that time, the sun will grow larger and eat up Mercury, Venus, and the Earth. This won't happen for a long time—about six billion years in the future!

Our **sun** is the closest thing to a perfect **SPHERE** that scientists have seen in nature.

SOLAR FLARES are giant explosions on **the sun's** surface.

The sun gives off **ULTRAVIOLET RAYS,** which human skin uses to manufacture **vitamin D** and help keep humans healthy. It's important to wear sunscreen because human skin can burn if exposed to too many ultraviolet rays.

The Latin word for **the sun** is **SOL.**

FACTS ABOUT BLACK HOLES

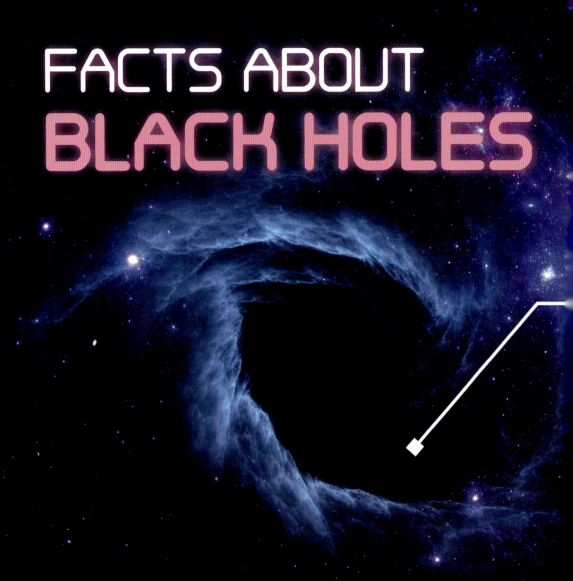

114

There are **MILLIONS** of black holes in the Milky Way galaxy.

Black holes are **DARK AREAS** with extremely powerful gravity that pull in anything that comes close. It is impossible to escape a black hole—even light can be pulled into it and trapped forever. Black holes can happen when a star is dying. Because no light can get out, people can't see black holes. They are **INVISIBLE.**

The surface of a black hole is called the **EVENT HORIZON.**

Black holes mainly consume **GAS** and **DUST,** but massive black holes can consume **ENTIRE STARS.**

Scientists captured the **FIRST PHOTOGRAPH** of a black hole in 2019 by linking together eight different giant telescopes.

The first black hole to be photographed is **6.5 BILLION** times the size of our sun.

If a human crossed a black hole's event horizon, they would be **SQUEEZED** and **STRETCHED,** like a noodle.

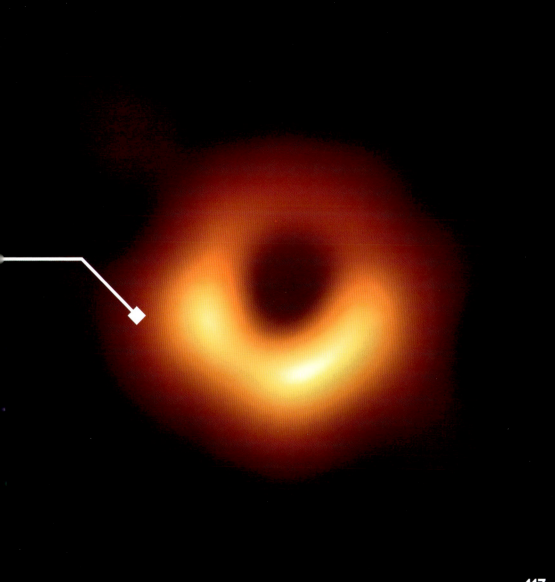

There are **FOUR** types of black holes: primordial, stellar, intermediate, and supermassive. A black hole's type is determined by its size.

While some black holes form when a star collapses, other black holes are **MYSTERIES.** For example, scientists still do not know for sure how supermassive black holes form because they are too large to have been formed by a dying star.

Astronomers believe there can also be **WHITE HOLES,** though one has never been found . . . yet. They believe a white hole would be the reverse of a black hole. It would expand outward and emit energy.

FACTS ABOUT TELESCOPES AND SATELLITES

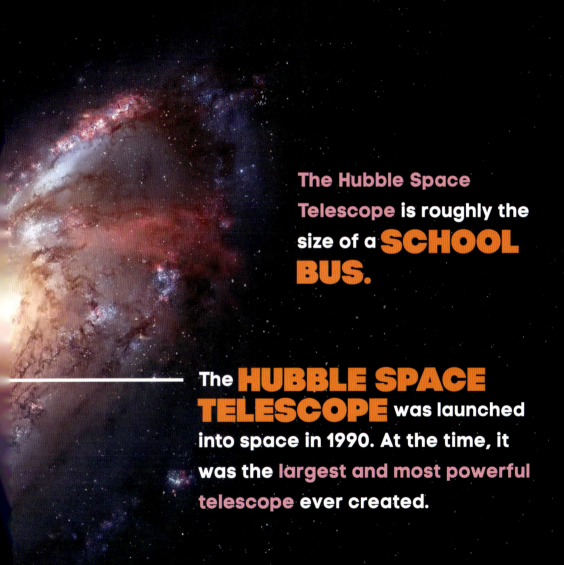

The Hubble Space Telescope is roughly the size of a SCHOOL BUS.

The **HUBBLE SPACE TELESCOPE** was launched into space in 1990. At the time, it was the largest and most powerful telescope ever created.

With the **Hubble Space Telescope** in space, scientists can explore the universe **TWENTY-FOUR HOURS** a day, **SEVEN DAYS** a week... all while staying on Earth.

The **Hubble Space Telescope** discovered **TWO MOONS** orbiting **Pluto** and allowed scientists to learn the age of the universe.

The **Hubble Space Telescope** has observed locations more than **13.4 BILLION** light-years away. This means the telescope has seen light that is billions of years old.

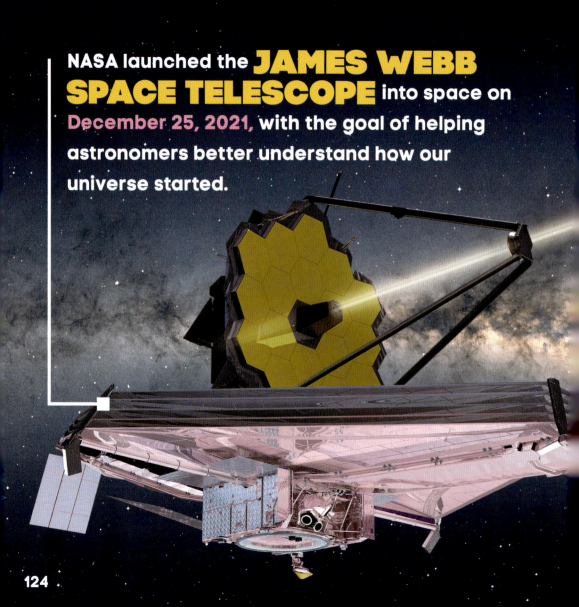

NASA launched the **JAMES WEBB SPACE TELESCOPE** into space on December 25, 2021, with the goal of helping astronomers better understand how our universe started.

The **James Webb Space Telescope** observes **INFRARED LIGHT,** which is a type of light humans cannot see.

The **James Webb Space Telescope** has special mirrors that allow it to see objects that are **NINE TIMES** fainter than the faintest object the Hubble Space Telescope can see.

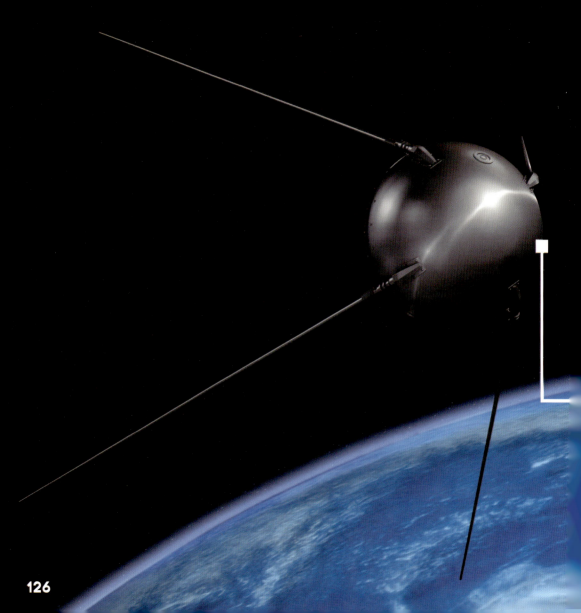

The **James Webb Space Telescope** can even see **EXOPLANETS,** which are planets outside of our immediate solar system.

A **SATELLITE** is a machine that humans launch into space. Once they are in space, satellites orbit around a planet or star. They mainly orbit around Earth.

The first-ever satellite in space was called **SPUTNIK,** launched by the Soviet Union in 1957. There are more than ten thousand satellites in space right now. Around nine thousand of them are active, and more than two thousand are floating around dead.

While some **satellites** take photos and explore space, others beam **TV SIGNALS** and **PHONE CALLS** around Earth.

The **VOYAGER 1 AND 2** space probes, launched by the USA in 1977, have observed **Jupiter, Saturn, Uranus,** and **Neptune.**

On board both the **Voyager 1 and 2 space probes** is a golden record containing nature sounds, music from various cultures, and spoken greetings from Earth-people in fifty-five different languages. This is so that **EXTRATERRESTRIAL BEINGS** can learn about Earth if they find the record out in the depths of space.

In 2012, the Voyager 1 space probe left our solar system and became the first spacecraft to enter **INTERSTELLAR SPACE.** Interstellar space is what we call the space beyond our solar system.

In 2018, the Voyager 2 space probe finally **JOINED** its twin spacecraft in exploring interstellar space.

As of today, NASA is still able to **COMMUNICATE** with the Voyager 2 space probe, and it is still considered active. *Hello out there, Voyager 2!*

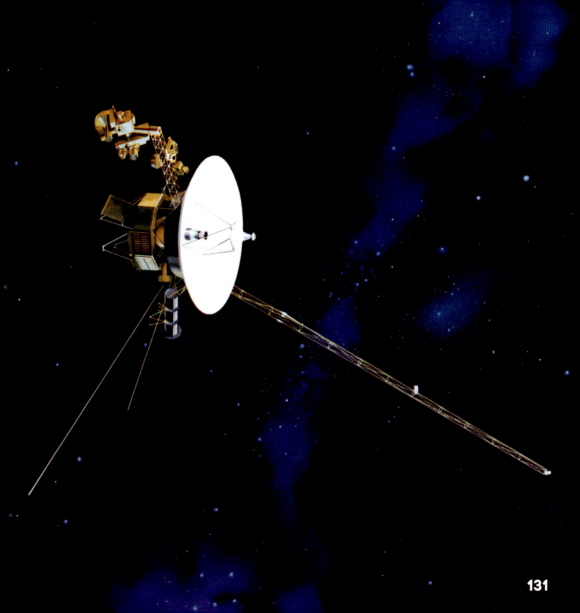

FACTS ABOUT STARS

Stars are giant balls of **PLASMA**, or intensely hot matter. There are billions of stars in the Milky Way galaxy, including our sun.

There are more **stars** in the
UNIVERSE than grains of
sand on all the beaches on Earth.

On a clear night, you can see around
TWO THOUSAND stars
from the Earth's surface.

When you look up at a **star**, you're seeing how it looked in the past. This is because its light has taken **THOUSANDS** of years to travel across space and reach your eyes.

The oldest dated **star** chart that historians have discovered came from **Ancient Egypt** in 1534 BC. That means it is more than **3,500** years old.

Stars are formed inside clouds made of dust and gas called **NEBULAE.**

Stars take **MILLIONS** of years to form, but they also live for millions of years.

When a **star** runs out of fuel, it sometimes explodes in what is known as a **SUPERNOVA.**

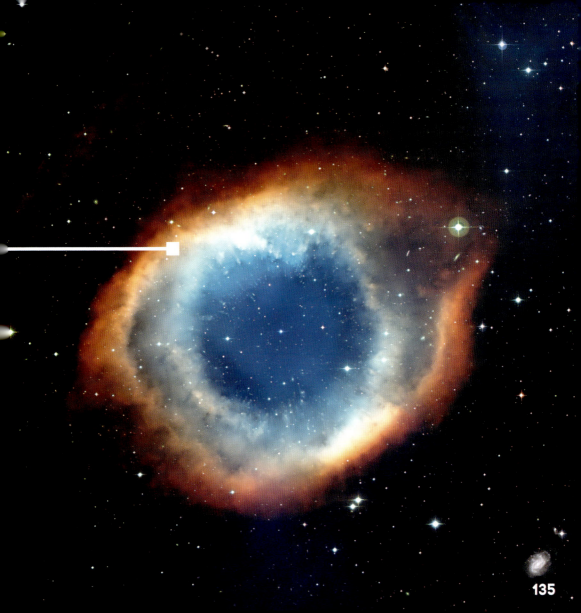

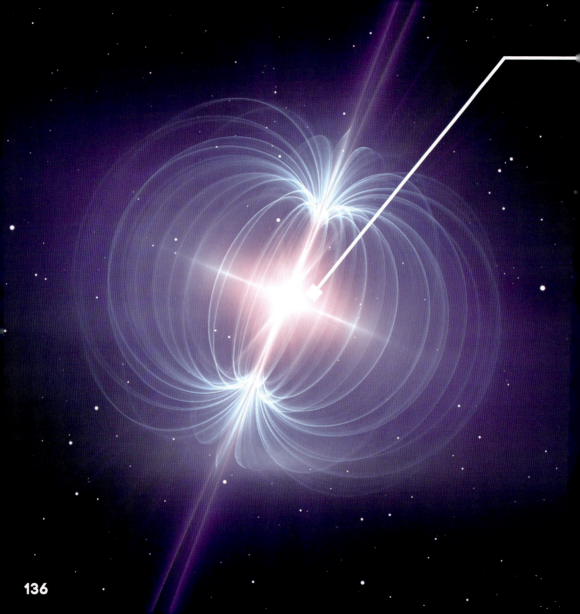

Following a supernova, some stars become **NEUTRON STARS.** Neutron stars are small and spherical. Because of how small they are, they are very hard to see. They emit light like other stars.

Neutron stars are only about thirteen miles wide but are incredibly **HEAVY.** A single spoonful of a neutron star would weigh more than all the humans on Earth.

Neutron stars can spin as fast as **SIX HUNDRED** times per second.

Stars shine in different colors based on their **TEMPERATURES:** blue, white, yellow, orange, and red.

Blue stars are the **HOTTEST,** burning at more than seventy thousand degrees Fahrenheit. **Red stars** are the **COOLEST,** with temperatures of around five thousand degrees Fahrenheit.

A **CONSTELLATION** is a large group of **stars** that form a pattern that we see from Earth.

There are **EIGHTY-EIGHT** officially recognized **constellations** found in our night sky.

The most recognizable **constellation** is called **ORION.** It is visible throughout most of the world.

THE BIG DIPPER is made up of *seven bright stars* and is one of the largest constellations. In the Northern Hemisphere, it can always be seen in the night sky. It looks like a big ladle—a deep spoon with a long handle.

In Latin, the word *constellation* means **"SET WITH STARS."**

THE LITTLE DIPPER is also made up of **seven stars.** At the end of its handle is Polaris, also known as the **NORTH STAR.**

Stars don't **TWINKLE.** The blinking is the star's light being disrupted by wind as it enters Earth's atmosphere.

FACTS ABOUT GALAXIES

Scientists believe the universe was created during an event called the **BIG BANG.**

It's believed that the universe began as just a single **POINT,** but during the big bang, it expanded and stretched to grow.

Ever since the big bang **13.8 BILLION** years ago, the universe has continued to expand.

Astronomers have no idea how **BIG** space is.

While the Earth orbits the sun, the sun (and all its planets) orbit the center of the Milky Way, which is a huge **BLACK HOLE.**

It takes our sun 225 million to 250 million years to orbit the center of the Milky Way. This length of time is called a **GALACTIC YEAR.**

Scientists have identified **FOUR** shapes of galaxies: elliptical, spiral, lenticular, and irregular.

A modern spacecraft would take **450 MILLION** years to reach the center of our galaxy from Earth.

The Milky Way's closest neighbor is the **ANDROMEDA GALAXY,** located 2.5 million light-years away. Scientists believe that in the next four billion years, the Milky Way and Andromeda galaxies will collide and form a **new galaxy.**

FACTS ABOUT SPACE JUNK

Humans have left **TWO HUNDRED TONS** of trash on the moon, including rocket boosters and nearly one hundred bags of human waste.

Because no one owns the moon, no one is officially **RESPONSIBLE** for cleaning it up.

There are more than **TWO HUNDRED THOUSAND** pieces of junk floating around in space.

Space junk orbits Earth at up to **EIGHTEEN THOUSAND** miles per hour.

In 2020, NASA created the **ARTEMIS ACCORDS,** a document of rules for cooperating peacefully in space. These accords have been signed by forty-three countries as of June 2024. The Artemis Accords include a rule about preventing any new, harmful space junk.

MORE FACTS ABOUT SPACE

LIGHTNING can happen in outer space. It's often seen on Earth, Jupiter, and Saturn.

In 2001, **Pizza Hut** delivered a **PIZZA** to the International Space Station by rocket.

If two pieces of the same type of **metal** touch in space, they will **FREEZE** together permanently.

A giant **WATER CLOUD** is floating through space twelve billion light-years away. It contains 140 trillion times the amount of water on Earth.

The **RADIO SIGNALS** used by spacecraft to contact Earth have about the same power as the light bulb found in a household refrigerator.

The Milky Way galaxy contains large amounts of a chemical called **ETHYL FORMATE,** which has a unique taste—it is similar to the flavor of raspberries. (But don't eat it!)

Not all planets stay in orbit around stars. There are trillions of planets that simply **DRIFT** around the galaxy.

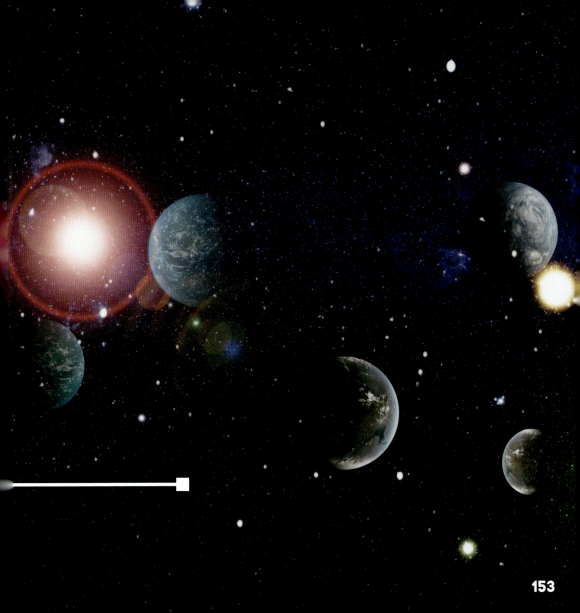

Any **liquids** released in outer space will form into a **SPHERE.** If someone cried tears into space, they'd all turn into tiny **floating balls.**

Scientists know more about the surfaces of **Mars** and **the moon** than they do about what is in Earth's **OCEANS.** There is a *lot* we don't know about life right here on Earth.

On a clear night, you can see up to **SEVEN** different galaxies from Earth's surface without a telescope.

The first foods to be eaten in outer space were **PUREED MEAT** and **CHOCOLATE**. The first soda to be consumed in outer space was **COCA-COLA.**

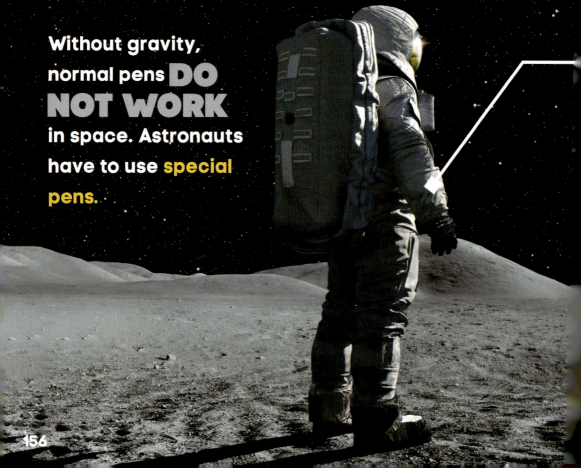

Astronauts cannot **BURP** in space. Without *gravity*, air can't rise from their stomachs.

Without gravity, normal pens **DO NOT WORK** in space. Astronauts have to use *special pens.*

A **BUZZ LIGHTYEAR** figure from the movie *Toy Story* once spent a year on the International Space Station. *"To infinity and beyond"* indeed!

Without a **space suit,** you would black out after just **FIFTEEN SECONDS** in space and be unable to function. A lot of movies that take place in space seem to ignore this fun fact!

In 2013, the **OLYMPIC TORCH** was transported to the International Space Station and was taken on a space walk. (The sports in the Olympics will remain on Earth, however.)

Thanks to space tourism, anyone can be an astronaut—but a ticket can cost up to **$55 MILLION.**

Scientists believe they have found an Earthlike planet about six hundred light-years away that could be habitable for humans. It is called **KEPLER-22 B.**

MORE INFORMATION

For more information about space, visit these websites:

NASA Space Place: spaceplace.nasa.gov

NASA Kids' Club: nasa.gov/learning-resources/nasa-kids-club

NASA+: plus.nasa.gov

NASA Exoplanets: exoplanets.nasa.gov

NASA Spot the Station (International Space Station tracker): spotthestation.nasa.gov/sightings/index.cfm

NASA Golden Record: voyager.jpl.nasa.gov/golden-record/whats-on-the-record

Every Satellite Orbiting Earth and Who Owns Them: dewesoft.com/blog/every-satellite-orbiting-earth-and-who-owns-them

TIME for Kids Space: timeforkids.com/g56/topics/space